UNSINKABLE *Lucile*

HOW A FARM GIRL BECAME THE QUEEN OF FASHION AND SURVIVED THE TITANIC

BY HUGH BREWSTER

ILLUSTRATED BY LAURIE McGAW

HISTORICAL CONSULTANT: RANDY BRYAN BIGHAM

FIREFLY BOOKS

Summer Hill

"Lucy Christiana, what on *earth!*" exclaimed Grandmama sternly from the porch. Lucy stood wet and shivering and muddy beside the farm pump while her mother filled a bucket.

"It was the boys —" Lucy began to say, but her grandmother interrupted.

"You mustn't blame others for your mischief, Lucy. Once you have changed your clothes, please come to the parlor."

Lucy knew what *that* meant — an hour of sitting in silence followed by a lecture on how young ladies ought to behave.

"The boys threw my hat in the duck pond," Lucy whimpered to her mother after Grandmama had left. "I had to rescue it."

"I fear you're becoming a terrible tomboy, Lucy," her mother replied. "This dress may be ruined."

"But Grandmama always —" Lucy protested bleatingly.

"I know, Lucy, I know," her mother interrupted as she rinsed out a muddy cloth. "But this is *her* house."

Lucy and her younger sister, Elinor, had lived at Summer Hill, their grandparents' farm near Guelph, for almost as long as Lucy could remember. Her father had died of typhoid in England when she was only two, and her mother then had little choice but to return to Canada with Lucy and baby Elinor.

Elinor was Grandmama's favorite. She was quiet and pretty and loved to sit and listen to her grandmother's tales of life in the Old Country. Grandmama would tell stories of elegant, candlelit evenings in stately homes staffed with dozens of uniformed servants. And she believed firmly that Old World standards of proper behavior must be maintained in this raw, new country.

When she and Grandpapa had first arrived in Canada as pioneer farmers over 30 years before, Grandmama's relatives in France had taken pity on their unfortunate cousin in the Canadian wilderness. Each year they sent a huge barrel to Guelph that contained luxuries like silk stockings, lace collars and even last year's Paris gowns. The arrival of *le tonneau bienvenue* (the welcome barrel) still caused great excitement at Summer Hill.

"The *tonneau* is here! Grandpapa's gone to the station to fetch it!" Lucy would tell Elinor breathlessly. The two sisters would dance with excitement as the lid of the barrel was pried off, and out would spill gowns made of silks and satins in the shimmering colors of butterfly wings. They conjured up a romantic world far from the rutted roads and endless winters of Guelph. The barrel sometimes contained bolts of cloth, and Lucy would use the scraps to make clothes for her dolls. Later, she began sewing clothes for her mother and sister.

Lucy's mother was an attractive young widow, and many suitors came calling at Summer Hill. But she wished to remain faithful to the memory of her late husband. One of the most persistent in his proposals of marriage was David Kennedy, an

elderly Scotsman with a gray beard who owned a nearby farm. Lucy's mother at first refused him, but after he promised to take her and the girls to live in Great Britain, she eventually consented to marry him. She had made a promise to her husband before he died that she would raise the girls in England.

"Mother looked very sad, I remember, on her wedding day," Lucy later wrote, "but I was jubilant at the thought of the voyage to England and the fact of leaving Grandmama."

Jersey

England was nothing like the fairytale land that Lucy and Elinor had imagined. The towns they passed through on the train were dirty and poor. In Scotland the skies were gray, and Mr. Kennedy's brother and his family were as cold as their big, gloomy house. Lucy's mother's relatives on the island of Jersey were far more welcoming. The family soon decided to rent a house on this British island just off the coast of France since living there was cheaper and the mild climate suited Mr. Kennedy's health.

Government House on Jersey was a stately home that was right out of one of Grandmama's stories. It was the residence of Sir William Norcott, the island's lieutenant-governor, and Lucy and Elinor soon befriended his daughter Ada. One day, when Lucy was 11, Ada had some exciting news.

"You'll never guess who's coming here to dinner," she said. "Lillie Langtry!"

"Lillie Langtry!" Lucy and Elinor repeated excitedly. "Can we see her? Oh, please, Ada! Please!"

Lillie was a Jersey girl who had married and moved to London. There, her remarkable beauty caught the eye of a famous artist who asked to paint her portrait. Soon other painters and photographers also wanted to capture Lillie's image. Before long, Lillie Langtry was the most famous beauty in England.

On the night that "the Jersey Lily," as she was known, was to appear at Government House, Lucy and Elinor hid in the cloakroom under a dressing table, peering through peepholes they had cut in its calico and muslin cover. Once Lillie Langtry entered the room, however, the girls' excitement gave them away, and the celebrated beauty

Every artist wanted to paint Lillie Langtry. She soon became a famous actress and starred in plays in Great Britain and the USA.

pulled them out from beneath their hideaway. The two sisters were a bit tongue-tied, but Lillie was gracious and stunningly lovely in her white silk gown.

The next day, the girls spied Mrs. Langtry walking in the town wearing black velvet and furs. Lucy drew a sketch of her, fixing this moment in her memory. It would inspire a black velvet gown she would make for the first ball she attended at Government House the year she turned 18.

A hand-tinted family photo shows Lucy (center), Elinor (at left) and their mother in a horse-drawn carriage on Jersey in 1878.

Government House

ST. SAVIOUR, JERSEY, CHANNEL ISLANDS, MAY 1881

The military ball was the grandest event held at Government House each year. The men of the local regiment looked splendid in their scarlet uniforms, and the ladies donned their most fashionable new gowns. Most wore white or pastel colors, but Lucy's black velvet gown made her a standout, setting off her porcelain complexion and red hair. She drew the eye of a handsome young army captain, who asked to dance with her again and again.

He soon called on her at home, and they took long walks together on the hills overlooking the sea. Within weeks, she had fallen in love. Then suddenly, without warning, he stopped seeing her. Lucy was terribly hurt. Ever defiant, she packed her bags and stormed off to stay with relatives in England.

"I must let him see that I did not care," Lucy later wrote. "So to this end I married the next man who asked me, and he happened to be James Stuart Wallace."

London

James Stuart Wallace proved to be a bad husband. After giving Lucy what she called, "the worst six years I ever knew," he abandoned her. At the age of 28, Lucy was left almost penniless with a young child to support. She was determined to divorce Wallace even though divorce was not considered respectable at the time.

Lucy soon moved into her mother's small London apartment but knew that she needed to find work. What could she do? Night after night she lay awake worrying about this. Then one day while making a little dress for her daughter, Esmé, she had a flash of inspiration.

"Whatever I could or could not do," she thought, "I could make clothes. I would be a dressmaker."

Not long after this, a friend came to call and mentioned that she needed a new tea gown for an upcoming

(Above) Lucy with baby Esmé in 1885.

> ## "I had a flash of inspiration. I could make clothes. I would be a dressmaker."
>
> —Lucy Wallace

weekend party at a grand country house. Tea gowns were flowing, pretty creations that fashionable women wore in the afternoon when tea was served. Lucy set to work creating a tea gown with soft, accordion-pleated folds. It drew admiring comments at the country house party, and before long every woman who had seen it wanted one like it. Soon Lucy had to hire an assistant to help her fill the demand, and her mother's London apartment was covered with cut-out sections of tea gowns.

Tea gowns were elegant but informal dresses for relaxed entertaining at home. They were worn without the constricting corsets that fashionable women were then required to wear. Romantic tea gowns would be an important part of Lucile's designs throughout her career.

Maison Lucile

OLD BURLINGTON STREET, LONDON, ENGLAND, 1893

Mrs. WALLACE.

Maison Lucile,

—:o:—

Modes,
Robes,
Corsets,
Tailor-made
Gowns,
Coats, Etc.

24, Old Burlington St.

Within a year Lucy had four assistants and a dress shop called Maison Lucile that soon became the talk of fashionable London. Lucy took great care that each gown she designed suited the personality of the woman who would be wearing it. She called them "personality frocks" and they became very popular. Lucy also thought it a shame that her lovely gowns were worn over the plain white undergarments that "proper" Victorian women were supposed to wear.

"So I started making underclothes as delicate as cobwebs and as beautifully tinted as flowers," she later recalled. "Half the women in London flocked to see them, though they had not the courage to buy them at first."

But when Lucy's gossamer creations were adopted by famous women like Lillie Langtry, others in London society soon followed.

(Above, left) An 1893 magazine advertisement for Maison Lucile.

(Opposite) Lucy shows a customer a tea gown while lingerie items are displayed on a nearby table.

Buckingham Palace

"Mrs. Elinor Glyn!" announced the court chamberlain.

Elinor did a deep curtsy before the Princess of Wales, who acknowledged her with a regal nod. Now came the tricky part. You could not turn your back on royalty, so Elinor had to walk backward out of the gilded room without tripping on the long train of her gown. Her sister, Lucy, had rehearsed this with her many times during fittings for her court presentation outfit. Lucy had outdone herself by creating for Elinor a breathtaking white satin gown trimmed with silver ribbon and edged with lace. A diamond tiara secured the three white ostrich feathers — required for a court presentation — atop her upswept red hair. Elinor dazzled that spring day, outshining even the young debutantes being presented for their entry into high society.

It was all rather bittersweet for Lucy. As a divorcée, she could not be presented at court. Nor was she invited to the grand balls and country house weekends that her sister enjoyed since her marriage to Clayton Glyn, an English country landowner. Instead, Lucy mingled with artists, writers and theater folk, whose company she preferred anyway.

"I met the most interesting people," she later recalled fondly.

17 Hanover Square

The next year Lucy moved her salon to a townhouse on London's posh Hanover Square. She covered the walls in gray silk and installed elegant chairs and couches where customers could sip tea while choosing clothes. This was a world away from the plain workshops of other designers. And instead of showing her gowns on stuffed dummies, Lucy taught her young shopgirls how to walk and turn and display clothes. She gave them exotic names like Corisande and Gamela, and soon they became celebrities in their own right as the world's first fashion models.

Lucy also began creating costumes for the London theater. At the time, most clothes worn on the stage were made of stiff brocades and velvets that Lucy described as hanging in "heavy, lifeless folds." By using lighter fabrics and dressing actresses in real clothes, Lucy helped transform costume design. Customers soon flocked to

Maison Lucile asking for the same clothes they had seen in popular plays.

Soon the theater inspired another notion. "Slowly the idea of a mannequin parade [fashion show], which would be as entertaining as any play, took shape in my mind," Lucy later recalled. "I would have glorious, goddess-like girls … displaying [my gowns] to the best advantage to an admiring audience of women. After I had visualized it all, the rest seemed possible."

What Lucy didn't know then was that this idea would change the fashion world forever.

(Above) This depiction of a Lucile salon in 1911 shows the same elegant style she established at 17 Hanover Square in 1897.

Lucy designed the gowns for the 1904 musical The Catch of the Season *and arranged for scenes from the show to be performed at her salon.*

The First Fashion Show

23 HANOVER SQUARE, LONDON, ENGLAND, 1904

Shortly after she had moved to an even larger salon on Hanover Square, Lucy sent out engraved invitations to her first fully staged mannequin parade. On April 28, 1904, a glittering crowd of elegant women — including Lillie Langtry, a princess and several duchesses — showed up to find Lucy's salon decorated with over 3,000 handmade silk roses. As the lights dimmed, a string orchestra began playing.

"I shall never forget the long-drawn breath of admiration," Lucy later wrote, "[when] the first of my glorious girls stepped upon the stage, pausing to show herself a moment before floating along the room to a burst of applause."

The next day the orders flowed in, and within months Lucy was putting on as many as three fashion shows a day. One newspaper dubbed Lucy's innovations "Lady Duff and Her Stuff," since by then she had acquired the title of Lady Duff Gordon.

Sir Cosmo Duff Gordon was a tall, reserved aristocrat who was a keen sportsman and a champion fencer. He was an early investor in Lucile Ltd but soon became captivated by Lucy herself. His mother, however, was fiercely opposed to her son marrying a divorcée, so they were not wed until after her death in 1900.

> *"There was never such a triumph for me as that wonderful afternoon."*
>
> —*Lucy Duff Gordon*

Crazy Big Hats

In 1907 Lucy designed the costumes for the actresses in the operetta *The Merry Widow*. The show was a smash hit and the large plumed hats she created for the singing star Lily Elsie (above) started a worldwide craze for big hats. "Every woman who wanted to be in the swim had to have a Merry Widow hat," Lucy recalled. "It carried the name of 'Lucile' all over Europe and the States." As other designers began imitating her, hats became bigger and bigger each year — making them the target of cartoons and comic postcards (opposite).

Say, honest, girls, it's beastly
To wear a thing like that,
And make us tag like pups, behind
Your MERRY WIDOW HAT.

No Admission
To the Surf---
The Merry Widow
Invades the Beach.

When Merry Widow hats
were offered as a giveaway
at a New York performance
of the operetta in June 1908,
it caused a stampede of
pushing and shoving, which
the *New York Times* dubbed,
"the Battle of the Hats."

◆

New York

(Left) Elinor Glyn.
(Right) Lucy Duff Gordon.

"Hey, Elinor Glyn, over here!" shouted the newspaper reporters gathered on the New York pier. Now a successful writer, Elinor had become world-famous because of her bestselling romance novel *Three Weeks.* For her arrival in New York, Elinor dressed like the heroine of her book in a purple Lucile outfit with matching hat and chiffon veil. Soon invitations to high-society parties began arriving at her suite at the Plaza Hotel. When Lucy heard of Elinor's success, she decided to join her in New York. The two famous sisters were invited everywhere — even to the White House in Washington where they met President Theodore Roosevelt. Lucy soon returned home, excited about opening a Lucile salon in New York. Elinor stayed on to promote her book, relieved at no longer having to share the spotlight with her sister.

When Lucy's New York shop opened in 1910, it was an immediate success. "Fashionable New York is in a flutter," one newspaper noted as lines formed before each fashion show.

"New York took me to its hospitable heart," Lucy later wrote in her memoir, "I became the rage."

Paris

Lucile's Paris salon.

After New York, Lucy decided to tackle Paris, the capital of world fashion. "Paris will teach her a lesson," was the sneering response from the French fashion world. But when Lucy opened with one of her unique fashion shows, her salon was mobbed. "We are sure," wrote one French fashion magazine, "that the dramatic performance with which Lady Duff Gordon startled Paris today will be copied by every designer here before long." This was a very sweet triumph for a girl from a Canadian farm who had once received castoff clothes from Paris. She decided to make Paris her headquarters and acquired an apartment near the Arc de Triomphe. It was there that she received a telegram in April of 1912 saying that she had to go to New York right away to sign the lease for a new, larger Lucile salon. "I booked a passage on the first available boat," Lucy later recalled. "The boat was the *Titanic*."

> ## "*I knew that I could convert Paris as I had converted New York.*"
>
> —*Lucy Duff Gordon*

A model displays a Lucile gown inside a French country house in a 1913 artist's portrayal.

◆

(Top) A label from one of her Paris gowns.
(Bottom) An illustration from a French
magazine depicts a 1911 Lucile fashion show.

On Board the Titanic

RMS TITANIC, APRIL 10–15, 1912

"I had never dreamt of traveling in such luxury," recalled Lucy of the *Titanic*. Everything about the ship delighted her — from her stateroom with its pink curtains to finding fresh strawberries on her breakfast plate. "Why you would think you were at the Ritz," she exclaimed to her husband, Cosmo. On the fifth night of the voyage, the weather suddenly turned cold, and Lucy decided to wear her fur coat over a stylish suit to dinner instead of an evening dress. There was talk of icebergs, but the mood in the ship's elegant à-la-carte restaurant was festive. The

Duff Gordons were joined by Lucy's secretary, Laura Mabel Francatelli, (who was nicknamed "Franks") and after dinner they sat by the fireplace in the first-class lounge. Cosmo soon went off to his stateroom for an early night, and Lucy sat chatting with Franks by the heater in her room before also turning in. After about an hour she was awakened by a rumbling noise deep beneath her. Suddenly the ship's engines stopped. Soon she heard people running on the deck outside her room. "We must have hit an iceberg," a voice exclaimed. "There is ice on the deck!"

Lucy's stateroom A-20.

Lucy walked across the hallway to her husband's stateroom and woke him with the news. "Don't be so ridiculous," he replied grumpily. "The worst that can happen is that it will slow us down. Go back to bed and don't worry." But Lucy *was* worried. She sat on her bed and listened to the sound of roaring steam being vented from the ship's funnels overhead. Then it stopped and she found the silence even more ominous. She went back to Cosmo's room. "I beg you to go up on deck and see what has happened!" she cried. Wearily, her husband dressed and left the room. Ten minutes later he was back, looking grave. He told Lucy she should dress warmly and prepare to go up to the top deck.

As Lucy was donning a fur coat over her silk dressing gown, Franks arrived from her room four decks below. "There is water in my cabin, and they are taking the covers off the lifeboats!" she announced breathlessly.

Just then a steward knocked on the door. "Sorry to alarm you, Madam, but the captain's orders are that all passengers are to put on lifebelts." He told them that women and children were being put into the boats for an hour or so, just as a precaution.

Cosmo soon arrived and led Lucy and Franks up the grand staircase. On hearing the call for ladies to

board, they stepped out onto the top deck where crewmen tried to pull the two women toward the boats. But Lucy refused to leave without Cosmo, and Franks clung to her. After three lifeboats had been lowered, the crowd on the deck dispersed, and Lucy noticed that a smaller boat was being prepared for loading.

Lucy pointed to the boat and asked Cosmo if they should try to get into it.

"We must wait for orders," he replied.

A few minutes later, however, Cosmo went forward and asked the officer if they could get in the boat.

"Yes, I wish you would," the ship's officer responded.

After the Duff Gordons and Franks had climbed into the lifeboat, the officer allowed two American men to board as well. He then put two crewmen in to handle the oars. Seeing no more passengers on the deck, he told five stokers who had come up from the lower depths of the ship that they could jump in too. He instructed the crewman in charge to row away from the ship and then stand by. On reaching the sea, however, the crewman was shocked to see water creeping toward the name *Titanic* on the bow and decided to row away quickly. In a lifeboat that could have carried 40 people, there were only 12.

A surviving Titanic lifebelt.

As they rowed toward a light on the horizon that never seemed to get any closer, Lucy was terribly seasick and lay stretched out and shivering in the lifeboat. In the distance, the *Titanic*'s stern rose ever higher against the starlit sky. They still heard snatches of music from the ship's orchestra drifting across the water and saw light streaming from every porthole. One row of shining windows disappeared. And then another. Lucy turned away, unable to look.

"My God! She is going now!" Cosmo suddenly cried out. There was a dull explosion as the giant liner broke in two. Lucy turned back to see the stern section of the ship rise up and stand motionless before it, too, plunged into the inky depths. She then heard what she called an "indescribable clamor" — the sound of over a thousand people dying in the freezing water. Eventually all was silent and Lucy lapsed into a kind of stupor interrupted by bouts of seasickness. As they rowed onward, she could make out the dark shapes of icebergs surrounding them.

(*Above*) *RMS* Carpathia.

(*Right*) Titanic *survivors on the deck of the* Carpathia.

Through the darkness, the RMS *Carpathia* raced to the *Titanic*'s rescue, arriving at dawn to see 18 small lifeboats and some floating wreckage — all that was left of the greatest ship in the world. Lucy's lifeboat was the second to arrive at the *Carpathia*, and she and Franks were hoisted up the side in bosun's chairs. Once on deck they "clung to each other like children," Lucy later wrote, "too exhausted to speak, only realizing the blessed fact that we were saved."

The Duff Gordons were given a cabin by kindly *Carpathia* passengers, and Lucy crawled into bed and fell into a deep sleep. She awoke to sunlight streaming in through the portholes and thought for a moment that she was still on the *Titanic*. Then memories of the disaster flooded back and she buried her face in the pillows and wept. Eventually she was able to dress and go up on deck where she encountered small groups of *Titanic* passengers, all of them discussing the tragedy. For the next three days as they steamed toward New York, the *Carpathia* was, in Lucy's words, "a ship of sorrow, as nearly all were grieving over the loss of somebody." The *Carpathia* had taken on board 712 survivors, fewer than a third of the 2,208 who had sailed on the *Titanic*'s maiden voyage.

On the evening of April 18, when the *Carpathia* arrived in New York harbor, a crowd of 40,000 people clogged lower Manhattan to greet the survivors. Throngs of newspaper reporters competed for scoops on "the story of the century." The Duff Gordons were met by friends and whisked off to a suite at the Ritz-Carlton Hotel where fresh clothes and flowers awaited them. Over dinner, Lucy gave a colorful account of their escape, which was relayed to a newspaper reporter — something she would live to regret. Three weeks later, the Duff Gordons returned to England and Lucy described the shocking scene that greeted them upon landing.

Lucy stands (third from left) beside Franks and in front of Cosmo in a photo taken on the Carpathia *of the survivors from her lifeboat. She brought her lifebelt and asked the others to sign it as a memento, and Sir Cosmo gave bank drafts to the crewmen to help replace their lost possessions. Unfortunately, this fueled gossip that "the lord and lady" had escaped in their own private boat by bribing the crewmen.*

Aftermath

"All over the station were newspaper placards — 'Duff Gordon Scandal'... 'Baronet and Wife Row Away from the Drowning'... " Lucy later recalled. "Newsboys ran by us shouting 'Read all about the *Titanic* coward.'"

The fact that a titled English couple had escaped in a boat only one-third full when so many passengers from the lower decks had perished was causing outrage. To make matters worse, a crewman in their lifeboat had testified at the British *Titanic* inquiry that Sir Cosmo and Her Ladyship had objected to going back to rescue those dying in the freezing water. This was not true, and Lucy and Cosmo soon decided to appear at the inquiry to clear their names.

When Lucy took the stand at the *Titanic* inquiry on May 20, 1912, she vigorously denied the crewman's claims. Lord Mersey, the head of the inquiry, would later write in his report that "the very gross charge" against the Duff Gordons was untrue. Yet, as Lucy later wrote, "a great deal of the mud that was flung stuck to us both. For myself, I did not mind ... but I minded very much for Cosmo's sake. The whole affair broke his heart and ruined his life."

Two years after the *Titanic* disaster, World War I broke out and the demand for fine gowns dwindled. Since the United States was not yet in the war, Lucy decided to make the New York salon her base in the hope that it could keep her business afloat. This succeeded better than she could have anticipated, and she soon opened a salon in Chicago that was her most lavish yet.

Fleurette's Dream

By 1917 Lucile was the most famous name in American fashion. She had a penthouse on Park Avenue and a beach house on Long Island Sound. Her articles in newspapers and magazines made her a fashion adviser to millions, and her clothes appeared in dozens of silent movies as well as on Broadway.

That year, her sister, Elinor, wrote to her from war-torn France where she was doing volunteer aid work. In a bombed-out village named Peronne, Elinor had seen a French family hiding in a cellar. Lying on a pile of sacks in a corner of the cellar was a beautiful young woman named Fleurette. Elinor discovered that before the war Fleurette had been a fashion model in Paris. When she suggested that her sister organize a New York fundraiser, Lucy's imagination was seized by Fleurette's story.

In December 1917 *Fleurette's Dream at Peronne*, a musical show featuring Lucy and her fashion models, drew sold-out crowds to New York's Palace Theater. It then went on a six-month, 16-city tour. In Washington, D.C., President Woodrow Wilson came backstage to compliment Lucy.

At the end of each show, Lucy appeared onstage with her chow dog, Mahmud, and made a plea for donations for French war relief. Soon she had raised enough money to rebuild Peronne and six other villages as well. Lucy thought that *Fleurette's Dream* was "the most beautiful thing I ever created." Years later, she told her grandson that standing before cheering audiences with her glorious girls arrayed behind her was the absolute peak of her career. The Canadian farm girl had come a long way.

Epilogue

By the time the *Fleurette's Dream* tour was over, Lucy was exhausted. The 1918 Spanish flu pandemic was raging, and friends of hers were dying. For the first time she lost interest in her business and decided to amalgamate it with another company. She agreed to stay on as chief designer, but this did not go well and by 1923 she was bankrupt.

Yet Lucy did not allow this to sink her. She returned to London and began designing clothes from her small apartment, much like she did when she started her career so many years before. One of her clients was her sister, Elinor, who was enjoying great success in Hollywood as a screenwriter and director.

In 1932 Lucy penned her autobiography, which became a bestseller. Two years later she was diagnosed with breast cancer, and

Lucy, aged 63.

on April 20, 1935, at the age of 71, Lucy died. She was buried alongside her late husband, Cosmo, even though they had lived apart in their later years. As time passed Lucy was best remembered for being a *Titanic* survivor, and portrayals of her appeared in books and movies about the disaster. Yet more recently she has been celebrated for her role as a fashion innovator, responsible for creating the first fashion shows and fashion models, and for helping to free women from the constricting corsets they were once required to wear.

"I have lived my life to its fullest extent," Lucy wrote in her memoir, "with many mistakes and with much payment for them. But I am still in love with life. I still think this world is a glorious place … and I am glad to have had the privilege of living."

"I have found satisfaction in creating a dream world of my own."
—Lucy Duff Gordon

(Top) Ballerina Anna Pavlova poses in her London garden in 1912 in a Lucile dress called "Blossoms of the Heart."
(Middle) A silk damask Lucile evening dress from 1919 is decorated with fabric flowers and silk ribbons.
(Bottom) This Lucile wedding gown made of satin and gauzy silk net and trimmed with lace was created for a 1916 New York society wedding.

The dreamy "Lucile look" was created with layers of chiffon, wisps of lace, shimmering silks and delicate embroidery. Some of her gowns can still be seen in museum collections today.

◆

GLOSSARY

bosun's chair: A swing-like device with a wooden or canvas seat, used to hoist a person up the side of a ship.

corset: A tight-fitting woman's undergarment worn to shape the figure.

debutante: A young woman, usually from a privileged family, who makes her formal entry or "debut" into society.

divorcée: A woman who is divorced. In the Victorian era, when divorce was less common than today, there was often disapproval of those who had been divorced.

funnels: The tall smokestacks on a steamship. The *Titanic* had four.

mannequin: A form representing the human body used to display clothes. Also an early name for a fashion model.

posh: Elegant or swanky.

presentation at court: A formal ceremony in which upper-class young women in England appeared before the sovereign to mark their entry into high society. Married women, such as Elinor Glyn, could also be presented at court. A court presentation gown was required to have a long train, and white plumes were worn on the head in honor of the emblem of the Prince of Wales.

Princess of Wales: The wife of the British heir to the throne. Princess Alexandra was standing in for Queen Victoria when Elinor Glyn was presented at court in 1896.

stokers: The men who shoveled coal into a ship's boilers to create the steam that drove the engines.

ABOUT THE AUTHOR, ILLUSTRATOR & HISTORIAN

Hugh Brewster spent his teen years in Guelph, Ontario, Canada, near Lucy's childhood home, Summer Hill. He is the author of 15 books for adults and young readers including a number of titles about the *Titanic*: *Inside the Titanic* (1997); *882½ Amazing Answers to All Your Questions About the Titanic* (with Laurie Coulter, 1999); *Deadly Voyage* (2011); and *Gilded Lives, Fatal Voyage* (2012). He lives in Toronto, Ontario.

Laurie McGaw has previously collaborated with Hugh Brewster on a number of award-winning illustrated books, including *Polar the Titanic Bear* (1994), *Journey to Ellis Island* (1998), *To Be A Princess* (2001) and *African Princess* (2004). She is a renowned portrait artist and has also created 35 coins for the Royal Canadian Mint. She lives in Guelph, Ontario.

Randy Bryan Bigham is widely recognized as the world's leading expert on Lucy, Lady Duff Gordon (Lucile). His 2012 book *LUCILE: Her Life By Design* is a definitive sourcebook on the designer and is illustrated with many photographs and artifacts from his personal collection. He lives near Dallas, Texas.

ACKNOWLEDGEMENTS

Hugh Brewster and Laurie McGaw would like to acknowledge the remarkable contribution to this book made by Randy Bryan Bigham, who generously shared his expertise and archival images and artifacts. For historical advice and images we would also like to thank Günter Bäbler, Mike Beatty, Ken Marschall, Tom Lyndsky, Julia Schloss and Marlis Schweitzer. Laurie McGaw would like to thank Katherine Turner and Scarborough Players, Barbara Bryce and Guelph Little Theatre for lending costumes for photo shoots, and Cidalia Melo of KKP Guelph for photocopy services. Thanks also to all those who posed: Ross, Gwynne and Owen Phillips; Rodrigo Fernandez-Stoll; Emily, James, Anita and Vicki Lamond; Briana Templeton; Mike Kiss; Kathleen Miller; Monika Grau; Bob Calwell; A.J. Facciclo; Sophia Rose; Janette Hayhoe; John Livernois; Sean Corner; Christopher, Melaya, Calvin and Emily Horsten; Kelly Hughes; Ian Conlon; Lauryn Conlon; Jack MacBrien; Nicole Wright; Edie Wright-Moragne; Rosie Tilley, Scarlett Slade and Elsje Roos.

PICTURE CREDITS

All original art is by Laurie McGaw. All archival images unless otherwise designated are courtesy of Randy Bryan Bigham.

Author's Collection: p.6; p.7 (Langtry); p.15.
Mike Beatty: Title page (right); p.26; p.28. back jacket (bottom right).
Division of Work and Industry, National Museum of American History, Smithsonian Institution; p.30; p.32 (bottom).
Gregg Jasper: p.22 (right); p.23 (inset).
Library of Congress Prints and Photographic Archive: p.22 (left); p. 32 (top).
Marlis Schweitzer: p. 20 (right); p.21 (middle and bottom).
The Henry Ford: p.39 (left, middle).
University of Guelph Library, Archives, and Special Collections, Regional History Collection XR1 MS A408: p.3.
Wellington County Museum & Archives, A2002.54, ph16847: p. 7 (bottom).

A FIREFLY BOOK

Published by Firefly Books Ltd. 2022
Copyright © 2022 Firefly Books Ltd.
Text copyright © 2022 Hugh Brewster
Illustrations copyright © 2022 Laurie McGaw
Design and compilation copyright © 2022 Whitfield Editions
Photographs copyright © as listed above.

First printing

Library of Congress Control Number: 2021948563

Library and Archives Canada Cataloguing in Publication
A CIP record for this title is available from Library and Archives Canada

Produced by Whitfield Editions
Photo colorization by Rick Kowalczykowski, Icon Photography Inc.
Design by Kevin Cockburn, PageWave Graphics Inc.
Color work by Colourgenics.

Published in the United States by
Firefly Books (U.S.) Inc.
P.O. Box 1338, Ellicott Station
Buffalo, New York 14205

Published in Canada by
Firefly Books Ltd.
50 Staples Avenue, Unit 1
Richmond Hill, Ontario L4B 0A7

Printed in China

Canada We acknowledge the financial support of the Government of Canada.